MY FIRST BOOK
ANIMALS

by Dee Phillips

MY FIRST BOOK OF
ANIMALS

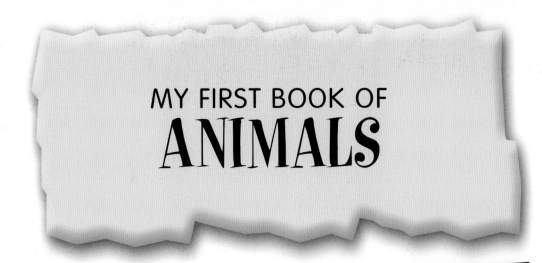

Copyright © **ticktock Entertainment Ltd 2008**

First published in Great Britain in 2008 by **ticktock Media Ltd.,**

The Old Sawmill, 103 Goods Station Road, Tunbridge Wells, Kent, TN1 2DP

ISBN-13 978 1 84696 787 0 pbk

Printed in China

9 8 7 6 5 4 3 2

Picture Credits: Brandon Cole Marine Photography/ Alamy: 52, 53, 57. Corbis: 41, 42. Michael & Patricia Fogden/ Minden Pictures/ FLPA: 70b. Stan Osolinski/ Photolibrary Group: 67. Oxford Scientific/ Photolibrary: 58c, 71. Shutterstock: OFC, 8, 9, 2, 32, 40, 43, , 8, 9, 6, 66, 68, 7, 83, 88, 89, 92-93. ticktock Media Ltd: 1-7, 9-18, 20-23, 2-3, 33-39, 45-47, 50-60, 62-65, 69-74, 76-82, 84-87, 90-91. All illustrations.

CONTENTS

Words that appear in **bold** are explained in the glossary.

MEET THE ANIMALS

Welcome to the world of animals, from tiny creepy-crawlies to soaring predators!

There are many different kinds of animals. In this book, you can discover **mammals**, birds, **reptiles**, **amphibians** and minibeasts. Animals live in many different places on Earth. Discover which animals live in the deep oceans, the icy cold of the Antarctic, on high mountains or even in the burning hot desert.

ANIMAL MENUS

Some animals, like tigers and alligators, only eat meat or fish.
Other animals, like giraffes and dung beetles, only eat plants.
Many animals, such as meerkats and chimpanzees,
like to eat meat and plants!

Look for these pictures in your book, and they will tell
you what kind of food each animal eats.

Plants

**Meat
(other animals
or bugs)**

**Fish or small
ocean creatures**

**Bugs or
spiders**

A WORLD OF ANIMALS
The map on this page shows our world

The different parts of the world are called continents. North America and Europe are both continents. Some of the animals in this book live in lots of places on just one continent. Other animals live on many different continents.

Some animals in this book only live in one country, such as America or Japan.

When you read about an animal in your book, see if you can find the place where they live on the map.

Can you point to the part of the world where you live?

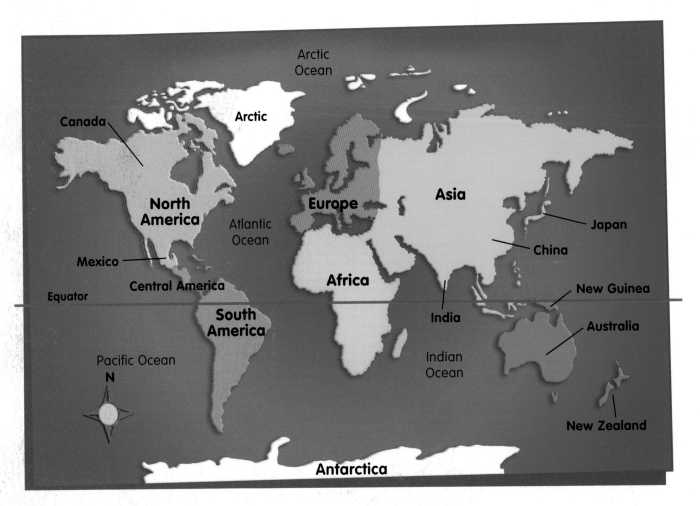

ANIMAL HABITATS

Some animals live in hot places, such as deserts, others live in forests or in the ocean. The different types of places where animals live are called **habitats**.

Look for these pictures in your book, and they will tell you what kind of habitat each animal lives in.

Deserts – hot, dry, sandy places where it hardly ever rains

Lakes, ponds, rivers or streams

Grasslands – dry places covered with grass

Rainforests – warm forests with lots of rain

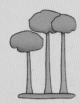

Temperate forests – cool forests with trees that lose their leaves in winter

Coniferous forests – cold forests with trees that stay green all year

Tropical waters – waters near the Equator

Polar regions – cold frozen places in the very north and south of the Earth

Mountains – high, rocky places

Oceans

Sea bed – the bottom of the ocean

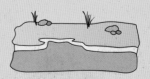

Seashores

CAMEL

Camels live in the **deserts** of Africa and Asia. They live in dry, sandy places where there is very little food or water.

A baby camel is called a **calf**.

Camels eat grass and plants.

There are two types of camels. Bactrian camels have two humps. Dromedaries have one hump.

— 5m

— 4m

— 3m

— 2m

— 1m

Camels store fat in their humps. They use the fat for energy when there is no food.

A camel can go without water for almost two weeks!

CHIMPANZEE

Chimpanzees are **apes**. They live in **forests** in Africa. Chimps eat fruit, leaves and bugs – like ants and **termites**.

Chimpanzees walk on all fours. Their arms are longer than their legs.

Chimps make faces to show other chimps that they are happy, frightened or angry!

This baby chimp needs his mum to do everything for him – just like you did!

Mother chimps feed, **groom** and carry their babies around until the babies are three or four years old.

ELEPHANT

Elephants live in Africa and Asia. They are the **biggest** animals that live on land.

Elephants live in **herds** of mums and babies.

A baby elephant is called a **calf**. Calves weigh over 100 kilograms when they are born!

2m   4m   6m   8m

Elephants eat grass, leaves, **roots**, branches, **bark** and fruit.

They drink enough water to fill a bathtub, every day!

Elephants use their trunks for smelling, picking up food and sucking up water.

These HUGE teeth are called **tusks**.

FRUIT BAT

Bats are **mammals** that fly! There are many different types, including lots of different fruit bats.

Fruit bats live in **forests** in Africa, Europe, Asia and Australia.

A baby bat is called a **pup**.

Fruit bats come in lots of sizes.

1m   2m   3m   4m

Fruit bats only eat the juice and the soft, squishy bits of fruit.

The bat's wings fold up.

This is a flying fox fruit bat

They search for food at night. During the day they rest, hanging upside down!

GIANT PANDA

Giant pandas live in just one small part of China, in Asia. They live high in the **mountains** in cold, wet **forests**.

Pandas eat bamboo – a tough, woody grass. They hold it in their front paws.

Pandas need to eat lots of bamboo to get all the energy they need. So they eat for up to 12 hours every day.

A baby panda is called a **cub**.

Cubs are blind, hairless and just 15 centimetres long when they are born.

GIRAFFE

Giraffes are the **tallest** animals in the world. They live on **grasslands** in Africa.

5m

4m

3m

Giraffes eat leaves and twigs.

2m

A giraffe's long neck and tongue help it reach leaves at the tops of trees. A giraffe's tongue can be 45 centimetres long!

1m

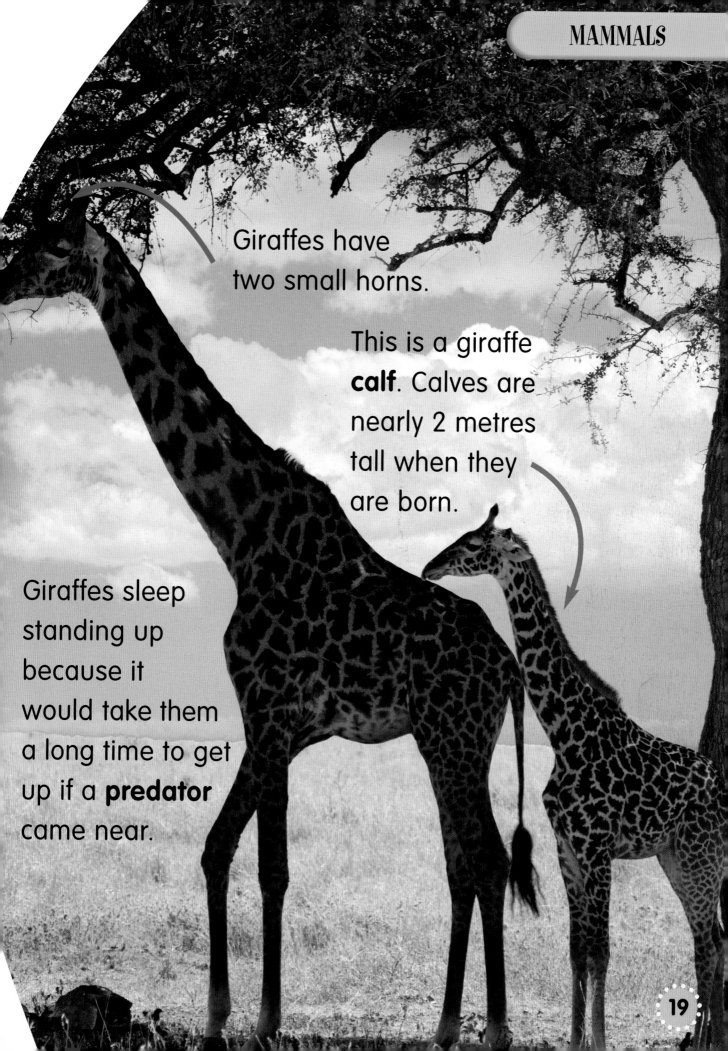

Giraffes have two small horns.

This is a giraffe **calf**. Calves are nearly 2 metres tall when they are born.

Giraffes sleep standing up because it would take them a long time to get up if a **predator** came near.

GORILLA

5m

4m

Gorillas are the **biggest** of all the **apes**. They live in **forests** in Africa. Gorillas eat plants and fruit.

3m

Grown-up male gorillas have silver-coloured fur on their backs. They are called silverbacks.

2m

1m

Gorillas live in family groups. The silverback is the leader of the family.

Grown-up gorillas teach the babies how to find food.

At night, gorillas build nests of branches and leaves to sleep in.

Gorillas are gentle and very clever. Baby gorillas like to play!

21

HIPPOPOTAMUS

Hippopotamuses live in **lakes**, rivers and **wetlands** in Africa. They have huge mouths and teeth, and can be very fierce.

Baby hippos are born underwater and can weigh up to 50 kilograms.

A baby hippo is called a **calf**.

1m   2m   3m   4m

A hippo can close its nostrils so water cannot get in!

Hippos live in **herds**.

Hippos spend most of the day in the water. At night they come out onto land to eat grass.

5m
4m
3m
2m
1m

KANGAROO

Kangaroos live on **grasslands** and in **forests** in Australia.

Kangaroos hop very fast using their big, strong back legs.

Their tails help them to balance.

A baby kangaroo is only 2 centimetres long when it is born. It lives and grows in its mum's special **pouch**. Animals that do this are called **marsupials**.

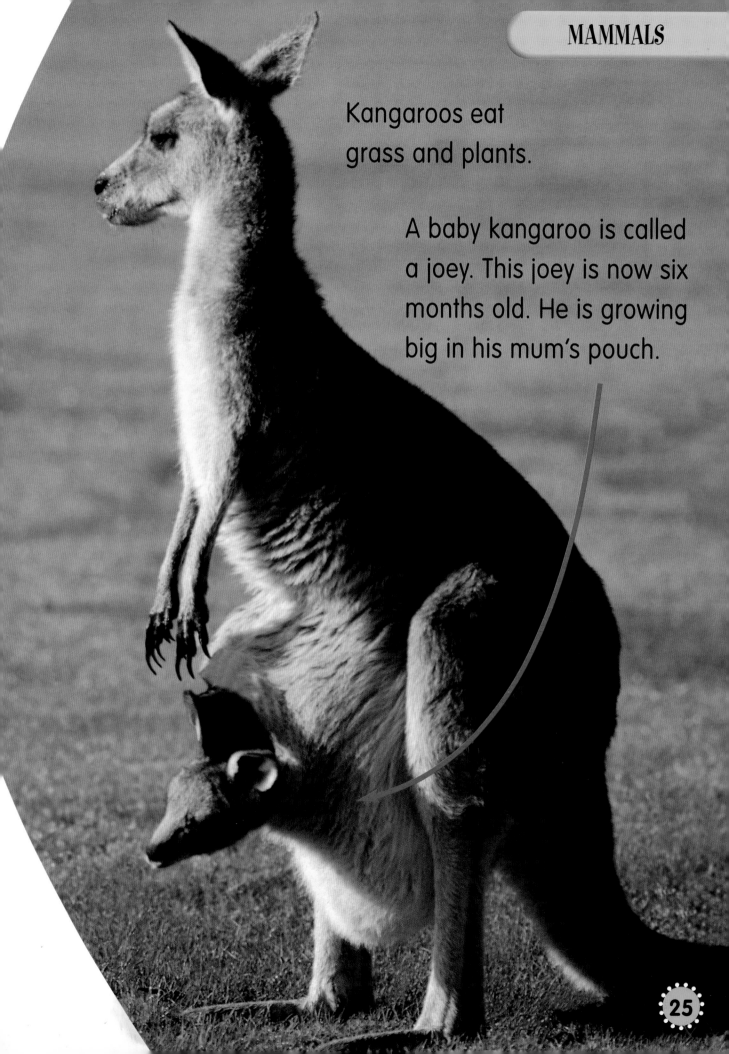

Kangaroos eat grass and plants.

A baby kangaroo is called a joey. This joey is now six months old. He is growing big in his mum's pouch.

LION

Lions are big, strong cats. They live in family groups called prides. These African lions live on **grasslands**.

The male lion has a thick, furry mane.

Females are called lionesses.

A male lion's ROAR can be heard 8 kilometres away.

1m   2m   3m   4m

Lions eat antelopes, **buffaloes** and zebras. Lion families hunt as a team!

This is a lion **cub**. All the lionesses in a pride help to look after each other's cubs.

MANDRILL

Mandrills are the **biggest** members of the **monkey** family. They live in **forests** in Africa.

This baby mandrill holds on to his mum's tummy. When he gets heavier, he will ride on her back.

Mandrills eat seeds, fruit, birds' eggs and small animals. They carry extra food in their cheek **pouches**.

5m

4m

3m

2m

1m

Mandrill families spend all day searching for food on the ground. At night, they sleep in trees.

Male mandrills have red and blue faces.

MEERKAT

Meerkats live on **grasslands** in Africa. They live in big groups in underground **burrows**.

Baby meerkats are called **pups**.

One grown-up meerkat babysits all the pups while the rest of the group goes to look for food.

Meerkat look-outs stand on high places and make a special noise if they see a **predator**.

Meerkats eat bugs, plants and small animals such as **lizards** and mice.

They have long claws for digging burrows and digging up bugs.

POLAR BEAR

Polar bears live in the Arctic on icy, cold land and on huge patches of frozen ocean.

A baby polar bear is called a **cub**. Mother polar bears dig **dens** in the snow, where they give birth to their cubs.

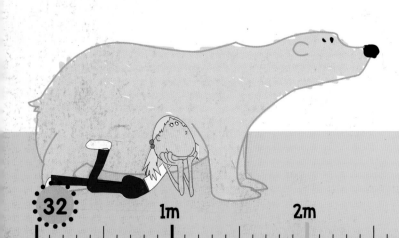

1m   2m   3m   4m

Polar bears are the biggest **predator** animal that lives on land. Their main food is seals.

Polar bears can smell food from almost two kilometres away!

They have thick fur and **blubber**.

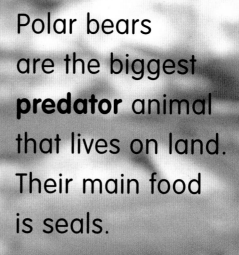

Their huge paws are the size of dinner plates!

RHINOCEROS

Rhinos are HUGE **mammals**. They live in **forests** and on **grasslands** in Africa and Asia. Rhinos eat grasses and plants.

There are five different kinds of rhino. The rhinos in this picture are White rhinos. They can weigh over 2 tonnes.

A baby rhinoceros is called a **calf**. Mum uses her horn to protect her calf from **predators**.

1m 2m 3m 4m

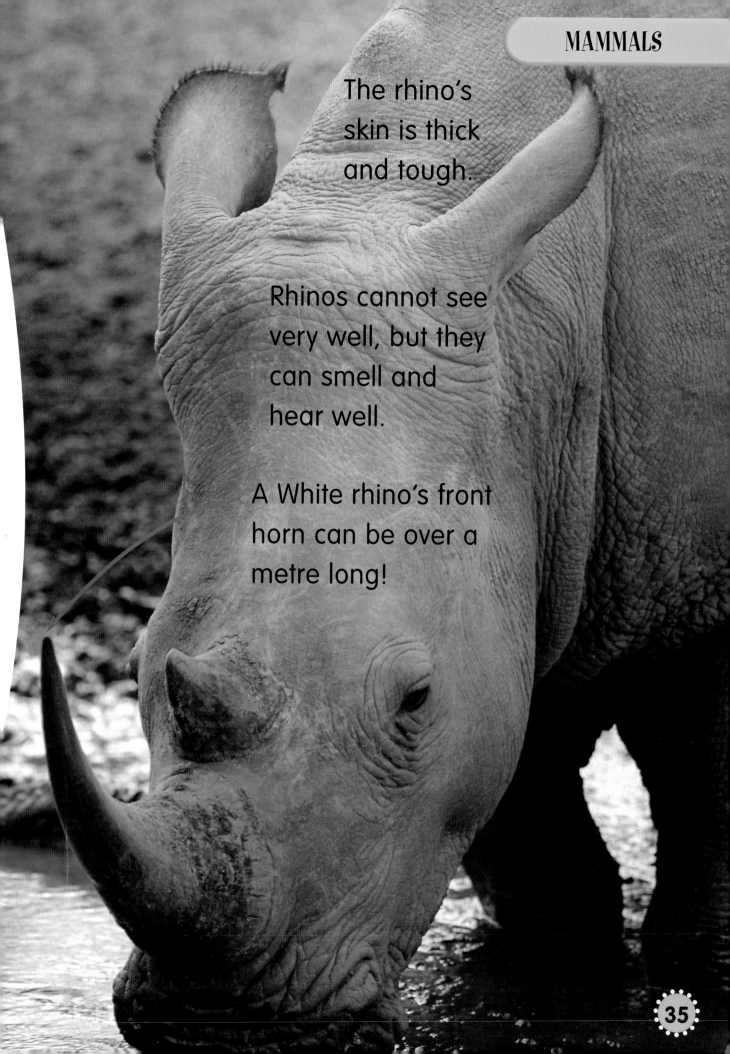

The rhino's skin is thick and tough.

Rhinos cannot see very well, but they can smell and hear well.

A White rhino's front horn can be over a metre long!

TIGER

Tigers are the **biggest** members of the cat family. They live in **forests** in Asia. Grown-up tigers normally live alone.

Tigers mainly hunt at night. They can catch big animals such as **deer** and antelopes.

Baby tigers are called **cubs**.

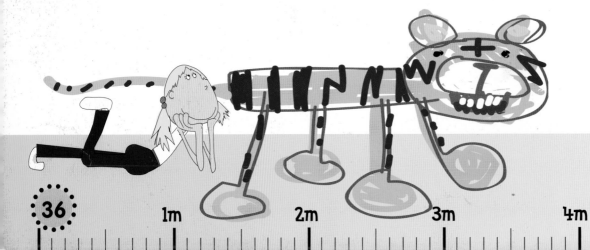

1m   2m   3m   4m

Some tigers live in hot places. They like to go swimming to keep cool. Other tigers live in cold, snowy places.

Tigers have black stripes. Every tiger's stripey pattern is different.

ZEBRA

Zebras are wild cousins of horses.
They live on **grasslands** in Africa,
and their main food is grass.

A baby zebra is called a **foal**.
The foal can stand up just a
few minutes after it is born!

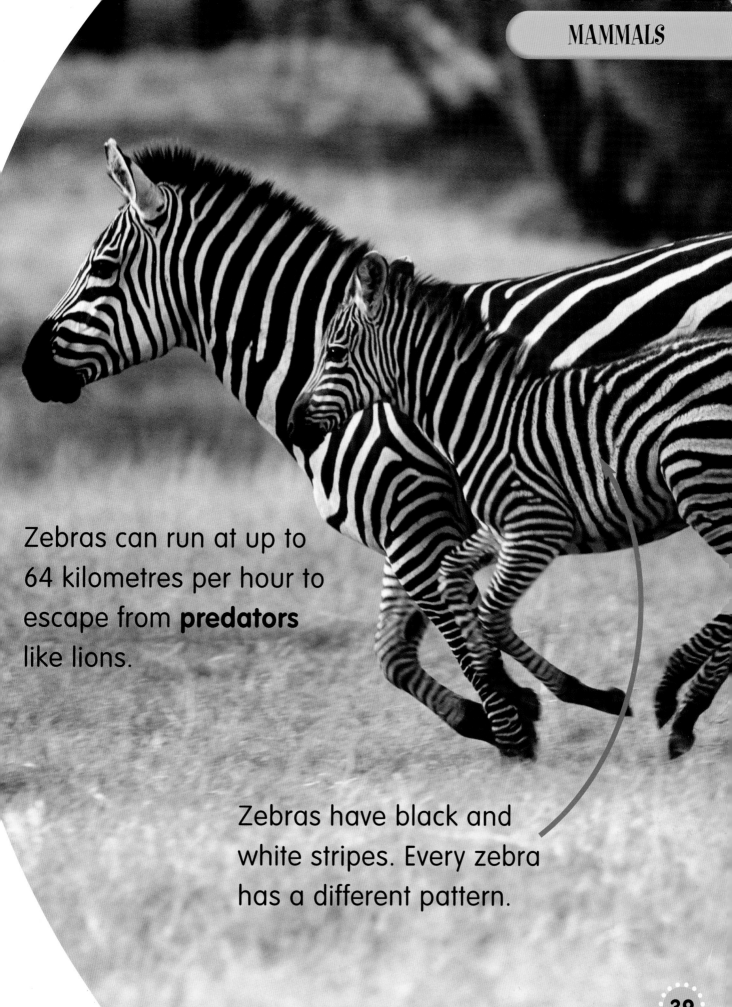

Zebras can run at up to 64 kilometres per hour to escape from **predators** like lions.

Zebras have black and white stripes. Every zebra has a different pattern.

BALD EAGLE

Bald eagles usually live near water. They grab fish from the surface with their claws. They also eat other birds, small mammals, **reptiles** and carrion (dead animals).

Bald eagles nest in high, hard-to-reach places. They use the same nest over and over, adding more branches and twigs every year.

The largest bald eagle nest ever found was 6.1 metres deep and 2.9 metres wide!

1m   2m   3m   4m

The bald eagle is the national bird of the USA.

OSTRICH

Ostriches live in large **herds**.

They cannot fly, but they can run

very fast – up to 70 kilometres per hour!

Ostrich eggs are about the size of a honeydew melon. That makes them the biggest egg in the animal kingdom.

When the eggs **hatch**, the father looks after the babies.

Ostriches are even bigger than your mum and dad. They are the world's biggest birds.

The ostrich's long, thin neck makes up almost half its height.

PENGUIN

Penguins are birds that are very good swimmers. They can survive in extremely cold places like the Antarctic.

They spend most of the time in the water catching fish, **krill** and squid to eat. Their wings are like flippers.

How **BIG** is an emperor **penguin?**

1.1 m   1 m

There are 17 **species** of penguin. The emperor penguin is the largest and lives in Antarctica.

Penguins are ideally suited to their environment. They have thousands of tiny feathers and a layer of fat under the skin.

BLUE WHALE

Blue whales are the **largest** animals that have ever lived on Earth. They live in all the oceans of the world.

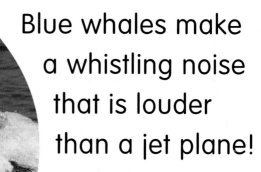

Blue whales make a whistling noise that is louder than a jet plane!

A blue whale's heart is the same size as a small car!

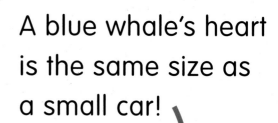

10m   20m   30m   40m

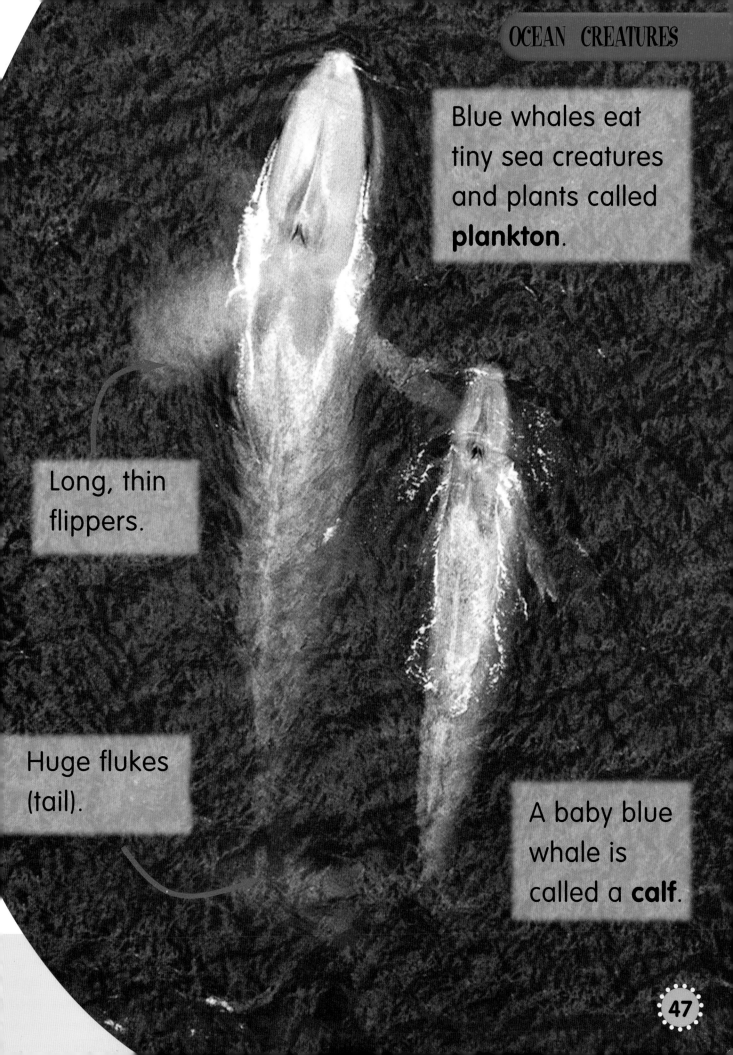

Blue whales eat tiny sea creatures and plants called **plankton**.

Long, thin flippers.

Huge flukes (tail).

A baby blue whale is called a **calf**.

CLOWNFISH

Clownfish are brightly-coloured little fish that live in sea anemones. They live in **tropical** oceans where the water is warm.

Clownfish hunt their **prey** by hiding among the anemone's **tentacles**. They have slime on their body that protects them from the anemone's stings.

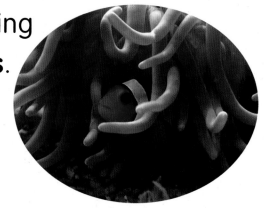

How **BIG** is a **clownfish?**

12 cm

1 m

Clownfish get their name from their bright markings. They look a bit like a clown!

Most clownfish live in pairs. They lay their eggs on rocks next to the anemone they live in.

DOLPHIN

Dolphins are **mammals** that live in the ocean and in some rivers. There are many different kinds of dolphin, and they come in lots of sizes!

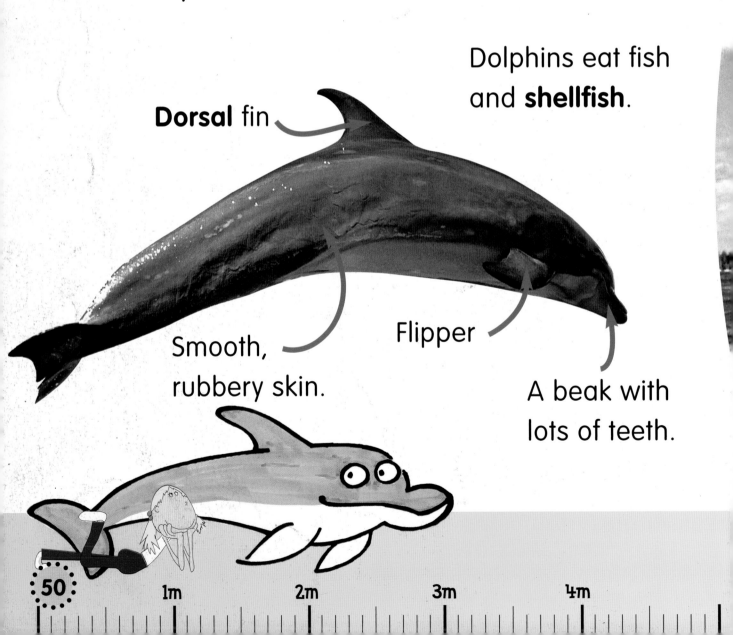

Dolphins eat fish and **shellfish**.

Dorsal fin

Smooth, rubbery skin.

Flipper

A beak with lots of teeth.

1m   2m   3m   4m

Baby dolphins are called **calves**. They drink milk from their mums under the water.

These bottlenose dolphins can leap 6 metres into the air!

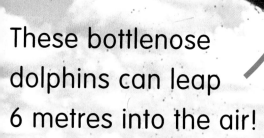

Dolphins live in groups called pods. They talk to each other using squeaky sounds.

GREAT WHITE SHARK

The great white shark is the most dangerous fish in the sea. It lives in warm and **tropical** waters.

The great white shark has strong jaws and rows of sharp teeth. It eats large fish, seabirds, seals and dolphins, and very rarely people.

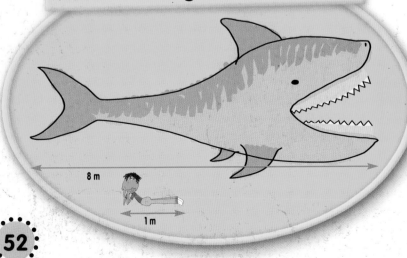

How **BIG** is a **great white shark?**

8 m

1 m

A great white shark has hundreds of teeth. They can each be up to 8 centimetres long.

The great white shark has good eyesight and an excellent sense of smell. It can smell food or a tiny drop of blood from a long way away.

HAMMERHEAD SHARK

The hammerhead shark's name comes from the shape of its head. It looks just like a hammer! The hammerhead shark lives in warm oceans.

The eyes and nostrils of the hammerhead shark are at the ends of its head. It has sharp, **serrated** teeth.

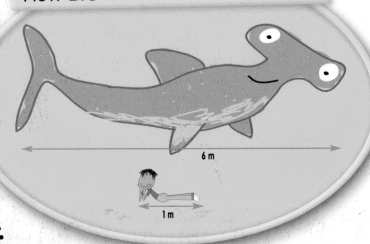

How **BIG** is a **hammerhead shark?**

6 m

1 m

Hammerhead sharks eat squid, octopuses, rays and **crustaceans**. They even eat other sharks.

There are five different **species** of hammerhead shark. All are very dangerous.

Hammerhead sharks give birth to between 20 and 40 live young. When they are born, they are about 70 centimetres long.

JELLYFISH

Jellyfish live in oceans all over the world. They have soft bodies and long, stinging **venomous tentacles**, which they use to catch fish.

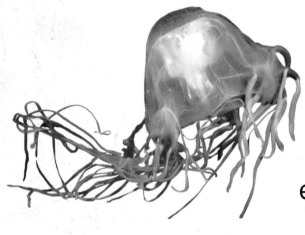

The box jellyfish is very pale, blue and transparent. This means you can't see it very well, even in clear water.

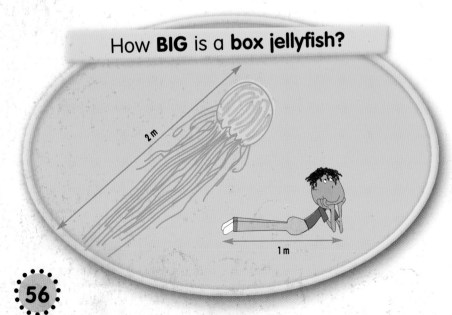

How **BIG** is a **box jellyfish?**

2 m

1 m

The sting of the box jellyfish is very strong, and can kill.

This is a cannonball jellyfish.

A jellyfish's body is shaped like a saucer and the mouth is underneath in the centre.

LOBSTER

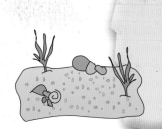

Lobsters are **marine crustaceans**. They are found in oceans all over the world. Females can lay up to 10,000 eggs at a time.

Lobsters carry on growing throughout their lives. They shed their old 'skin' as they outgrow it.

How **BIG** is a **lobster?**

50 cm

1 m

The lobster is protected by a hard **exoskeleton** on the outside of its body.

Lobsters have five pairs of jointed legs. The first have large, pincer-like claws that they use to crush their **prey**.

Lobsters are **scavengers** and will eat whatever they find. They particularly like shellfish and may attack live fish.

OCTOPUS

Octopuses have eight **tentacles** or arms that are covered in suckers. They use these to catch fish and **crustaceans** to eat.

There are 100 different **species** of octopuses. The largest is this giant Pacific octopus (at 5 metres).

How **BIG** is a **blue ringed octopus**?

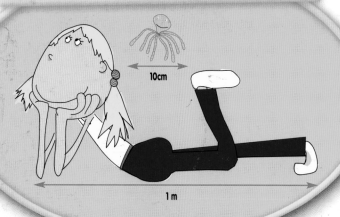

10cm

1 m

There are two different kinds of blue-ringed octopus. Each has a **venomous** sting.

When resting, the blue-ringed octopus
is pale brown or yellow. It only shows
its blue colour when it
feels threatened.

Octopuses can squirt black inky
liquid. This can blind their **predators**
and help them escape.

ORCA

The orca is found in oceans all over the world but prefers colder seas to the warmer waters near the Equator. It is also known as a killer whale.

The orca is a **mammal** and the largest type of dolphin. It gives birth to live young.

How **BIG** is a **killer whale?**

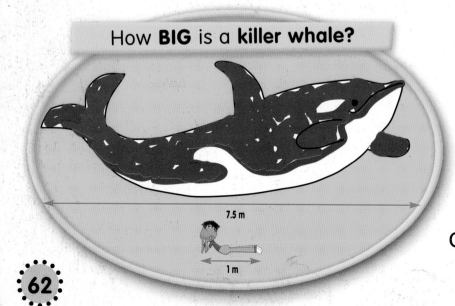

7.5 m

1 m

The orca has distinctive black and white colouring and a tall **dorsal** fin.

Like dolphins, orcas like to live in a group, called a 'pod'.

The orca eats fish, squid and seals, as well as larger animals like porpoises and small sharks.

SEAHORSE

Seahorses are small, bony fish that live in warm water. They have curly tails that they use to cling to seaweed.

Seahorses swim very slowly. They can change their colour to match their surroundings and hide from **predators**.

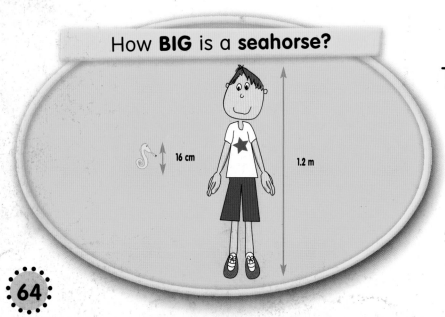

How **BIG** is a **seahorse?**

16 cm

1.2 m

The female produces eggs. Then they are held inside the male's body until they **hatch**.

The body of a seahorse is covered with tiny armoured plates instead of **scales**.

There are 34 different **species** of seahorse.

ALLIGATOR

Alligators are very big **reptiles** that spend a lot of time in the water. They float about in **lakes**, rivers and **swamps**. There are two types of alligator: American and Chinese.

There are up to 70 teeth in here.

Alligators have webbed feet for swimming.

Alligators hunt for fish, **snakes**, turtles, **lizards** and birds. They gobble up their **prey** whole.

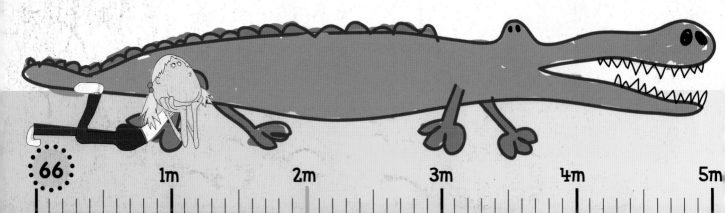

1m   2m   3m   4m   5m

The **hatchlings** call out "PEEP PEEP" to their mum as they **hatch**.

The mother carries the tiny hatchlings to the water on her back.

CHAMELEON

Chameleons are **lizards** with special skin. It can change colour if they get angry or excited. It can also allow them to blend in with their environment.

Chameleons use their long tongue to catch food. They shoot it out very quickly and insects get stuck to it.

A chameleon's tongue is longer than its body!

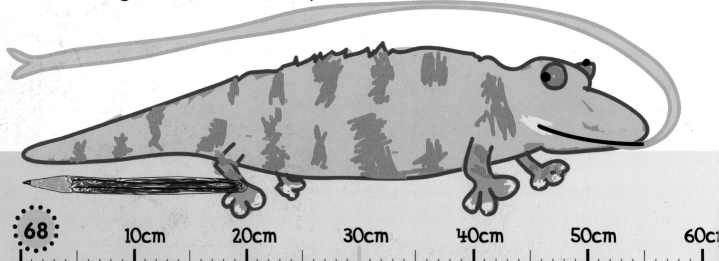

This is a Jackson's chameleon. It lives in east Africa and Hawaii.

One eye can look forwards, while the other eye is looking backwards.

COBRA

Cobras are **snakes** that live in lots of different **habitats** in south east Asia and Africa. They are very **venomous**.

These markings on the back of the hood look a bit like eyes.

When the cobra meets an enemy, it rears up and spreads this hood of skin.

The spitting cobra spits venom from its **fangs**. The **poison** can hit **prey** 2 metres away.

1m   2m   3m   4m   5m

Cobras eat rats, birds, **lizards**, toads and other snakes.

Indian cobras lay about 12–20 eggs. The baby snakes **hatch** after 60 days.

CROCODILE

Crocodiles are huge **reptiles**. They are **predators**. Crocodiles live in Africa, Australia and south east Asia in **lakes**, rivers and **swamps**.

Crocodiles eat lots of fish. Sometimes they catch and eat big animals such as **buffaloes**.

Mum crocodiles lay their eggs in a hole on the sandy riverbank.

They have thick skin with **scales**.

1m   2m   3m   4m   5m   6m   7m   8m   9m

A crocodile egg is about twice the size of a chicken egg.

Baby crocodiles hide in their mum's mouth if there is any danger.

KOMODO DRAGON

The giant Komodo dragon is the biggest of all the **lizards**. Komodo dragons live on **islands** near south east Asia.

They can smell food from up to 10 kilometres away and often eat other animals' leftover meat.

The Komodo has a deadly bite from the **poisonous** bacteria in its saliva.

1m   2m   3m   4m   5m

Mum dragons dig out large **burrows** in sandy ground for their eggs.

When the babies **hatch**, they live up in the trees to stay away from **predators**.

MARINE IGUANA

Marine iguanas, like land iguanas, are a type of **lizard**. They live on a group of **islands** called the Galapagos, which is off the west coast of Ecuador in South America.

Marine iguanas eat **algae** which grows on rocks near the shore.

They can remain underwater for up to an hour, although 5–10 minutes is more usual.

How **BIG** is a **marine iguana?**

75cm

1 m

Males are more brightly coloured than females, with red and green coloured backs.

When males fight, they put their heads together and push their enemy backwards. The loser has to retreat.

PYTHON

Pythons are all **snakes** which loop their bodies around their **prey** and squeeze to kill it. None are **venomous**.

They can swallow a **deer** whole.

The reticulated python (above) is the world's longest snake. Some have grown as big as 10 metres.

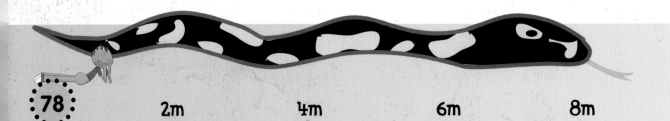

2m   4m   6m   8m   10m

There are 26 known **species** of python.
This is a green tree python.

Python mums lay between 15–100
eggs. Mums keep the eggs warm
with their bodies until the eggs **hatch**.

EUROPEAN COMMON FROG

The European common frog is the most common frog in northern Europe. It lives close to **lakes**, ponds, rivers and streams.

Frog mums lay thousands of eggs in one go. The eggs are called frogspawn. They look like a big clump of jelly.

The baby frogs are called tadpoles. They hatch after about two weeks, if the weather is warm enough.

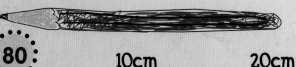

10cm   20cm   30cm   40cm   50cm

Frogs catch bugs to eat on their long, sticky tongues.

They spend most of their lives on land, and return to the water to breed.

TREE FROG

Tree frogs live in Australia, New Guinea, Europe America and Asia. There are many different types of tree frogs.

Tree frogs have sticky pads on their fingers and toes to help them climb trees.

Tree frogs usually come out at night looking for bugs to eat.

10cm   20cm   30cm   40cm   50cm

Giant tree frogs are the largest type of tree frog. They can grow to about 12 cm.

Mum frogs lay their eggs in water. The White's tree frog lays up to 3,000 eggs at one time.

DUNG BEETLE

Dung beetles come out at night. Different kinds of dung beetles eat the dung of different animals.

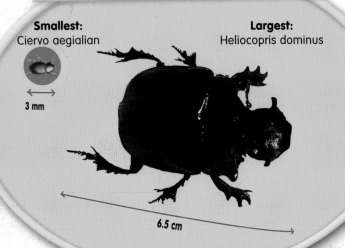

hard wing cases

Some dung beetles are very strong. They can roll a ball of dung 50 times their own weight.

How **BIG** is a **dung beetle?**

Smallest:
Ciervo aegialian

3 mm

Largest:
Heliocopris dominus

6.5 cm

six hairy legs

Some female dung beetles lay their eggs in a ball of dung to keep them safe. When the **larvae hatch**, they have food waiting for them!

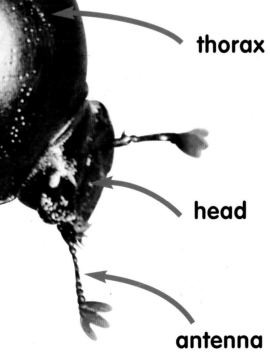

thorax

head

antenna

Dung Beetle Life Cycle

The female dung beetle lays an egg

A larva hatches from the egg

When fully grown the larva turns into a **pupa**

A dung beetle hatches from the pupa

GIANT MILLIPEDE

Millipede means 'thousand legs' but none have this many. Some have as few as 24 and others have up to 750 legs. They live on the ground and hide under stones and dead leaves. Millipedes mainly come out at night.

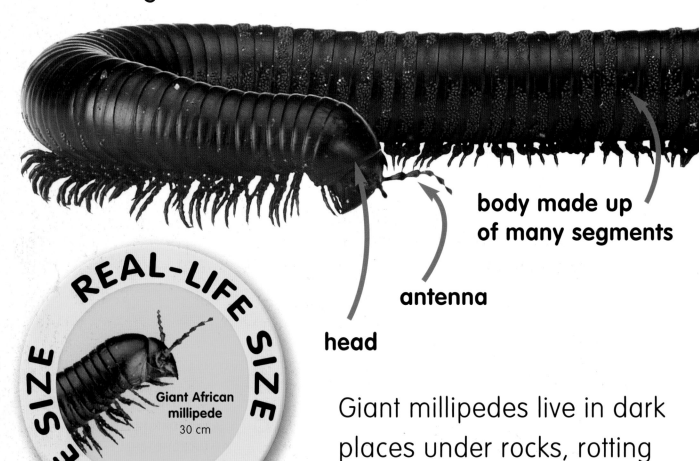

body made up
of many segments

antenna

head

REAL-LIFE SIZE

REAL-LIFE SIZE

Giant African
millipede
30 cm

Giant millipedes live in dark places under rocks, rotting logs, or fallen leaves. They cannot see very well.

If a millipede senses danger, it curls up so that its head and soft underside are protected.

four legs on each body segment

Giant Millipede Life Cycle

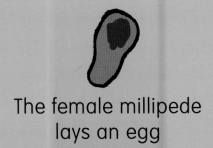

The female millipede lays an egg

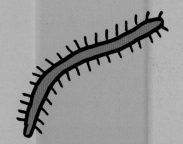

A young millipede **hatches** from the egg

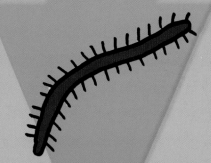

The young millipede grows up to be an adult

LADYBIRD
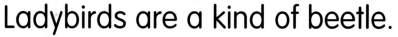

Ladybirds are a kind of beetle. They help protect gardens by eating tiny pests called aphids.

Ladybirds have hard **wing cases** to protect their wings. The bright colour tells birds, "I taste bad. Don't eat me!"

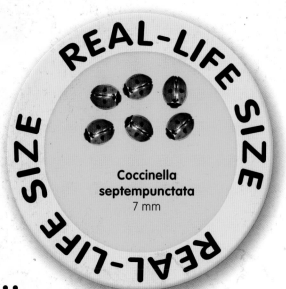

REAL-LIFE SIZE
REAL-LIFE SIZE

Coccinella
septempunctata
7 mm

wings fold
up when
not in use

hard wing
case

leg

antenna

head

When it is cold, ladybirds huddle together to keep warm. During the winter, they **hibernate** under logs, leaves or **bark**.

Ladybird Life Cycle

A female ladybird lays an egg

A **larva hatches** from the egg

When fully grown the larva becomes a **pupa**

A ladybird hatches from the pupa

PRAYING MANTID

Praying mantids belong to the cockroach family. Their large eyes help them spot their **prey**. They eat other insects, such as beetles and butterflies.

A praying mantid whips out its spiky front legs to grab other insects. The spikes help it hold its wiggling prey while the mantid starts eating!

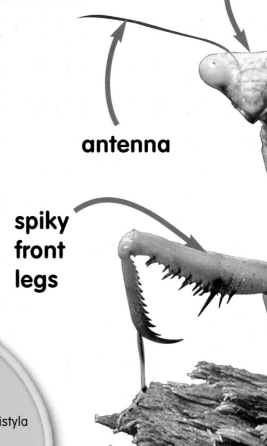

head

antenna

spiky front legs

How **BIG** is a **praying mantid**?

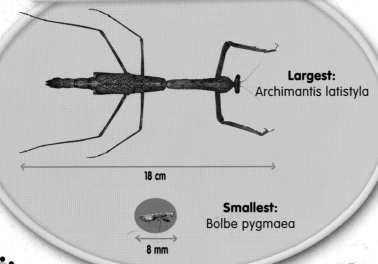

Largest:
Archimantis latistyla

18 cm

Smallest:
Bolbe pygmaea

8 mm

When a praying mantid is about to grab a meal, it holds its front legs up as if it were praying.

abdomen

Praying Mantid Life Cycle

The female mantid lays an egg

A **nymph hatches** out of the egg

The nymph develops into an adult mantid

TARANTULA

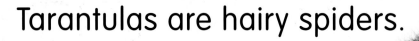

Tarantulas are hairy spiders. Most are very large. They use sharp **fangs** to kill insects, **lizards**, frogs, small birds and even **snakes**.

abdomen

strong jaws

one of two pedipalps, used to hold on to prey

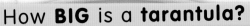

How **BIG** is a **tarantula?**

5 mm
Smallest:
Spruce fir moss spider

Largest:
Goliath tarantula

28 cm

Tarantulas have a deadly bite that sends **venom** into their **prey**.

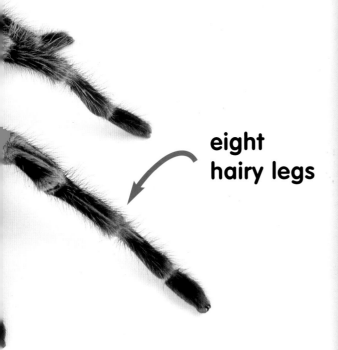

eight hairy legs

Tarantulas do not make a web. They hunt their prey on the ground.

Tarantula Life Cycle

The female tarantula lays an egg

A spiderling **hatches** from the egg

The spiderling grows into an adult tarantula

93

Glossary

Algae Group of simple, non-flowering plants, like seaweed.

Amphibians Animals that spend part of their time in water and part on land. Amphibians lay their eggs in water. Frogs, toads, newts and salamanders are amphibians.

Apes Animals from the primate family (which includes monkeys, humans and lemurs). Apes and monkeys look a bit alike, but while most monkeys have tails, apes don't.

Bark The tough, outer covering of tree trunks and tree branches.

Blubber A thick layer of fat under the skin.

Buffaloes Big, plant-eating wild animals that look a bit like cows. Buffaloes can be two metres tall.

Burrows Holes or tunnels that animals dig as homes.

Calf (Calves) The name for the babies of antelopes, buffaloes, whales, camels, dolphins, elephants, giraffes, hippos, deer, rhinos and walruses.

Crustacean An animal with jointed legs and a hard shell, including crabs, lobsters and shrimps.

Cubs The name for the babies of giant pandas, lions, polar bears and tigers.

Deer A family of plant-eating animals. The males normally have antlers.

Dens The homes of wild animals.

Deserts Places where hardly any rain falls. Many lizards and snakes live in deserts, even though they are hot, dry places.

Dorsal On the back, especially with regard to fins.

Exoskeleton A hard outer covering of an animal that supports or protects it.

Fangs Very sharp teeth. Snakes' fangs are hollow (like drinking straws) and are used to inject venom into their prey.

Forests Places where there are lots of trees.

Grasslands Dry places covered with grass, with very few bushes or trees.

Groom When an animal cleans itself and takes care of its fur or hair.

Habitats Different types of places around the world, such as forests, deserts and grasslands.

Hatch To be born by breaking out of an egg.

Hatchlings The name for the babies of some reptiles. They are called hatchlings because they hatch from eggs.

Herds Large groups of animals.

Hibernate To spend the winter sleeping in a burrow (or other warm, safe place) while there is not much food around.

Islands Small areas of land completely surrounded by ocean.

Krill Tiny, shrimp-like ocean creatures that are eaten by whales and other animals.

Lakes Large areas of inland water.

Larvae The name for the babies of creatures such as bugs and newts. These animals start as eggs; they hatch out as larvae and then grow and change into grown-ups.

Lizards Reptiles with scaly skin and legs. Some lizards are tiny, while others such as the Komodo dragon (see page 74) are huge.

Mammals Animals with fur or hair that give birth to live babies and feed them milk.

Marine Anything relating to the sea.

Marsupials Mammals that carry their newborn babies in a pouch until the babies are big enough to look after themselves. Kangaroos are marsupials.

Monkeys Animals from the primate family (which includes apes, humans and lemurs). Monkeys and apes look a bit alike, but while most monkeys have tails, apes don't.

Mountains Large, rocky areas of land that are much higher than the surrounding area.

Nymph The young of certain kinds of insects. They hatch from an egg looking like a smaller version of their parents.

Plankton Tiny animals and plants that float and drift in open water and are a source of food for other marine life.

Poisonous The word we use to describe something that can kill when eaten.

Pouch (Pouches) A kind of pocket, made of skin, on the front of a marsupial animal; also a place for storing food inside an animal's cheeks.

Predators Animals that live by hunting and eating other animals.

Prey An animal that is hunted by another animal for food.

Pupa The stage of some insects' lives between larva and adulthood. The insect goes through major changes while closed up in a shell or coccoon.

Pups The name for the babies of bats, meerkats and seals.

Rainforests Warm, jungle-like forests with very tall trees and lots of plants and animals.

Reptiles Animals such as snakes, lizards, tortoises and turtles. They are cold-blooded and have scaly skin. Some reptiles lay eggs and some give birth to live babies.

Roots The part of a plant that is under the ground.

Scales Tough, flat sections of skin on the bodies of reptiles. They are made of the same stuff as your fingernails and toenails.

Scavenger An animal that feeds off waste and leftovers, rather than hunting itself.

Serrated Something with a jagged edge; saw-like.

Shallow When something, such as water, is not very deep.

Snakes Long, thin reptiles with scaly skin and no legs.

Species A group of animals that share the same TREE FROG characteristics.

Swamps Places where there is a lot of water or mud, and the ground is soft, wet and very squishy.

Tentacle Long flexible organ used for holding, feeling or moving.

Termites Small bugs that live in huge colonies (groups). They build mountain-shaped nests.

Territory The area where an animal lives. Animals guard their territories to stop other animals eating the food in the territory or taking the best places to sleep.

Tropical Relating to certain hot parts of the world.

Tusks Long, pointed teeth that grow out of an animal's face or mouth.

Venom Something that can make a person or animal very ill and even kill them. Some animals have venom inside their bodies that they use for killing their prey.

Venomous Producing a poisonous fluid injected by a bite or sting.

Wetlands Places where there is lots of water, such as ponds and streams, and where water plants grow.

Wing cases The hard front wings of beetles that fold over and protect the lower, flying wings.

Index